THE CHILI COOKBOOK

Tasty and easy recipes
of the southwest.

THE CHILI COOKBOOK

TASTE OF THE SOUTHWEST

By
Savour Press
Copyright © by Wentworth Publishing House
All rights reserved

Published by
Savour Press, a DBA of Wentworth Publishing House

Let's get it started!

Welcome to Savour.

You might be wondering what is in chili that make it as one of American's favorite dishes. Chili comes in a variety of recipes and variation, depending on your preference, such as vegetarian chili, pork or beef chili. If you run out of ideas what to serve for your dinner, especially in winter, why not cook a chili dish?

As a comfort food, it gives you full satisfaction as the taste is super yummy, whatever recipe you have chosen. As soon as you have started cooking a chili recipe, the urge to cook another chili dish keeps haunting you. This is because, chilis are easy to do while it fills your hungry stomach.

Don't fret when a surprise guest comes to your home, Savour has a lot to offer from Flatlander Chili to Lobster Chili. All you have to do is to have enough stocks of chili ingredients, spices, beans along with meat and vegetables in your pantry, so no need to rush to the supermarket to buy the stuffs. Try our 20 chili recipes that are divided into different chapters for your convenience. Enjoy cooking!

About This Book

Cooking is not just a household chore in today's generation. This has become a passion and an outlet for some people who want to prove themselves that they can be an excellent cook, rather than a simple eater. That's what Savour wants you to know. This is why; this book is created to open up your mind about cooking. This book ushers you to a wide variety of chili recipes for the winter and tailgating. Whether you are a vegetarian, a Paleo advocate, a meat eater, we have prepared wide selections of chili recipes that you can share with your guests and loved ones. With the infusion of beef, chili, spicy ingredients, vegetables and beans, you will get an idea as to how chilis are cooked, and how easy to do. Have fun and get ready for your turn in the kitchen!

TABLE OF CONTENTS

INTRODUCTION

A lot has been said about chili recipes. Yes, we love chilis prepared in a nearby restaurant. But eating them outside of your home could be tricky, since we do not know how they are prepared; whether they are loaded with ingredients that are unfit to your family's health. There has been a wide debate as to the origin of chilis, if they come from Mexico or in Texas. Whatever it is, we have chili recipes, especially created to give you full satisfaction while feeling lonely during a cold evening, or watching your favorite football team. This eBook has everything you need to start your experiment in the kitchen. People who have tried our 20 recipes rave about their delectable taste, even non-Americans love them with much gusto.

Enjoy!

CHAPTER 1: BEEF

FLATLANDER CHILI

You will surely love the thick sauce of this chili recipe, an infusion of thick tomato sauce, tomato juice, red beans, ground meat and spices. Not only a good source of beta carotene, this chili will fill your stomach while tailgating or attending an outdoor concert.

Servings: 10

Ingredients

2 pounds ground **lean beef**

1 can (46 ounces) **tomato juice**

1 can (29 ounces) **tomato sauce**

1 ½ cups finely chopped **onion**

½ cup finely chopped **celery**

¼ cup finely chopped **green bell pepper**

¼ cup **chili powder**

1 teaspoon **salt**

2 teaspoons ground **cumin**

1 ½ teaspoons **garlic powder**

½ teaspoon ground **black pepper**

½ teaspoon **white sugar**

1/8 teaspoon ground **cayenne pepper**

½ teaspoon dried **oregano**

2 cups (canned) drained **red beans**

DIRECTIONS:

In a deep skillet, place the ground beef and cook on medium-high heat. Stir until golden brown.

Remove excess oil, crumble the meat and set aside.

In another deep skillet, place the cooked beef together with the remaining ingredients.

Bring to a boil. Stir mixture and simmer over low heat for 1 to ½ hours.

Enjoy!

Nutritional Information: 347 calories; 19.9 g fat; 68 mg cholesterol; 22.6 g carbohydrates; 21.4 g protein; 1246 mg sodium.

POLISH CHILI

What makes this chili interesting is the infusion of Polish sausage, beef, fresh tomatoes and chilis, so that every bite is always a memorable experience.

Servings: 12

Ingredients

2 pounds **ground beef**

1 pound chopped cooked **Polish sausage** or **kielbasa**

1 large chopped **onion**

3 minced **garlic cloves**

4 chopped **Anaheim chilies** (stemmed and seeded)

3 seeded and chopped **jalapeno peppers**

3 **yellow wax peppers** (seeded and chopped)

4 chopped medium size **tomatoes**

4 husked and chopped **tomatillos**

½ cup distilled **white vinegar**

¼ cup **tomato sauce**

1 jar (4 ounces) jar drained and chopped **pimentos**

1 can of (15 ounces) drained and rinsed **pinto beans**

1 can of (15 ounces) drained and rinsed **kidney beans**

Directions

In a deep large pot, place the ground beef and cook over medium-high heat. Stirring constantly to crumble meat and pink color is gone. Drain off excess fat.

In the same pot, add the sausage, onion, garlic and stir fry until onion is translucent.

Add Anaheim, jalapeno and yellow wax peppers, tomatillos and tomatoes.

Stir mixture and simmer over medium heat for 20 minutes.

Pour vinegar, pimentos, and tomato sauce into the mixture, stir and add the kidney and pinto beans.

Cover chili mixture and simmer for 30 minutes over medium heat.

Enjoy!

Nutritional Information: 435 calories; 31.1 g fat; 89 mg cholesterol;   17.3 g carbohydrates; 21.7 g protein; 575 mg sodium.

SPICY ONION BEER CHILI

This recipe tastes so good, thanks to the beer, beef and onion infusion. Without beer in the recipe, you may name it as plain spicy onion chili.

Servings: 8

Ingredients

2 pounds ground **beef chuck**

2 large chopped **white onions**

2 cans (14.5 ounces) diced **tomatoes with juice**

2 cans (15 ounces) **tomato sauce**

1 can (12 ounces) **beer**

2 cans (15 ounces) **spicy chili beans**

¼ cup **Worcestershire sauce**

3 tablespoons **hot pepper sauce**

1/3 cup **chili powder**

4 fresh seeded and chopped **jalapeno peppers**

3 tablespoons **red pepper flakes**

Directions

Place ground beef chuck into a saucepan and cook on medium heat.

Stir occasionally to crumble beef until browned. Remove excess oil. Transfer crumbled beef into a large saucepan.

Add tomatoes, tomato sauce, onions, chili beans, and beer.

Season the mixture with Worcestershire sauce, chili powder, jalapeno, red pepper flakes, and hot pepper sauce.

Cover the saucepan, and simmer on low fire for two hours.

Remove saucepan from heat and cool.

Refrigerate the chili for two days to make it more flavorful. Reheat before serving.

Enjoy!

Nutritional Information: 369 calories; 14.2 g fat; 52 mg cholesterol;40 g carbohydrates; 23.2 g protein; 1395 mg sodium.

Blue Ribbon Chili

If you want the best hot chili, try this recipe that goes well with cornbread or crackers and hot coffee. This is the tastiest chili for the rainy days.

Servings: 8

Ingredients

2 pounds **ground beef**

½ chopped **onion**

1 teaspoon ground **black pepper**

2 ½ cups **tomato sauce**

1 jar (8 ounces) **salsa**

4 tablespoons **chili seasoning mix**

½ teaspoon **garlic salt**

1 can (15 ounces) **light red kidney beans**

1 can (15 ounces) **dark red kidney beans**

Directions

Combine ground beef and onion in a large saucepan.

Sauté over medium heat for 10 minutes until the meat is browned and onion is transparent. Remove excess oil.

Season beef with ground black pepper, garlic salt, chili seasoning mix, salsa and tomato sauce, stir mixture.

Add dark and light red kidney beans; stir to incorporate in the meat mixture.

Simmer chili over low fire for 1 hour, stirring occasionally.

Serve!

Nutritional Information: : 480 calories; 31.1 g fat; 96 mg cholesterol;24.9 g carbohydrates; 26.7 g protein; 1366 mg sodium.

One-Pot Chili Mac and Cheese

Simply prepared chili in one sitting, this recipe does not need to use numerous kitchen gadgets to come up with a yummy treat for tailgating.

Servings: 6

Ingredients

1 tablespoon **extra-virgin olive oil**

1 pound lean **ground beef**

3 minced **cloves garlic**

1 medium diced **sweet onion**

2 cups low-sodium **chicken broth**

2 cups **pasta sauce**

1 can (10 ounces) diced **tomatoes with green chili peppers**

1 can (16 ounces) undrained **mild chili beans**

1 1/2 cups uncooked **elbow macaroni**

1 teaspoon **chili powder**

1 teaspoon **cumin**

Salt and ground **black pepper** to taste

3/4 cup shredded **Cheddar cheese**

1/4 cup finely chopped fresh **parsley**

Directions

In a large cooking pot or Dutch oven, heat olive oil over medium-high heat.

Stir in onion, garlic, and ground beef; stir occasionally until meat is browned and crumbly for 3 minutes. Remove excess fat.

Add chicken broth, pasta sauce, beans, chili powder, cumin and the diced tomatoes with mild green chilies.

Add salt and pepper. Bring mixture to a boil and add in the pasta. Stir and cover.

Simmer chili and continue cooking until pasta is cooked per cooking instruction for 14 minutes over low fire.

Remove chili from heat. Add cheese and parsley, stir to combine.

Serve hot with additional parsley and cheese for toppings.

Serve!

Nutritional Information: 463 calories; 19.2 g fat; 66 mg cholesterol 45.9 g carbohydrates; 28.5 g protein; 1233 mg sodium.

CHAPTER 2: TURKEY

TURKEY CHILI

Have a hearty dinner with this simple and flavorful chili recipe. This is best served with sour cream, cheddar cheese and crackers, with fruit juice.

Servings: 8

Ingredients

1 pound **ground turkey**

1 ½ teaspoons **olive oil**

1 chopped **onion**

1 tablespoon minced **garlic**

2 cups **water**

1 can (28 ounces) crushed **tomatoes**

1 can (16 ounces) **kidney beans** (drained, rinsed and mashed)

1/2 teaspoon **salt**

2 tablespoons **chili powder**

1/2 teaspoon ground **black pepper**

1/2 teaspoon paprika1/2 teaspoon **oregano**, dried

1/2 teaspoon ground **cayenne pepper**

1/2 teaspoon ground **cumin**

Directions

In a large saucepan, heat oil over medium heat.

Place ground turkey in the saucepan, and cook until golden brown.

Stir in onion until transparent.

Add water into the turkey, stir in tomatoes, garlic and kidney beans.

Season browned turkey with salt, pepper, chili powder, oregano, paprika, cumin, cayenne pepper, and black pepper.

Bring mixture to a boil and simmer over low heat for 30 minutes.

Enjoy!

Nutritional Information: 185 calories; 6.1 g fat; 42 mg cholesterol;18.8 g carbohydrates; 16.4 g protein; 450 mg sodium.

SLOW COOKER TURKEY CHILI

Have a delicious dinner without feeling guilty with this recipe that does not make you fat at all. It is a good source of Vitamin C and lycopene to maintain a whistle-bait figure.

Servings: 8

Ingredients

2 pounds **ground turkey** (99% fat-free)

5 minced **cloves garlic**

1 tablespoon **olive oil**

1 chopped **green bell pepper**

1 chopped **red bell pepper**

2 chopped **jalapenos**

1 can (28 ounces) no salt added crushed **tomatoes**

1 can (15 ounces) no salt added diced **petite tomatoes**

1 can (15 ounces) drained and rinsed no salt added **kidney beans**

3 tablespoons **tomato paste**

½ teaspoon **hot sauce**

1 packet **stevia**

1/8 teaspoon **cayenne pepper**

3 tablespoons **chili powder**

1 ½ teaspoon **sea salt**

2 teaspoons **oregano**

Pinch of **pepper**

Directions

Heat olive oil in a saucepan and sauté garlic and onion for three minutes until translucent.

Stir in ground turkey and cook until brown and crumbly. Remove excess liquid if needed.

Add the remaining ingredients and stir occasionally.

Cover and cook mixture over medium-low heat for 1 hour.

Serve!

Nutritional Information: 262 calories; 3.6 g fat; 0 mg cholesterol; 25.9 g carbohydrates; 34.6 g protein; 4.8 g sugar.

CHAPTER 3: VEGETABLES

EASY VEGETARIAN CHILI

Next we have concocted an easy version of vegetarian chili. You have the option to add vegetables of your choice and throw them into the pot.

Servings: 8

Ingredients

1 tablespoon **vegetable oil**

1 cup chopped **onions**

3 cloves minced **garlic**

3/4 cup **carrots**, chopped

1 cup green **bell pepper**, chopped

1 cup red **bell pepper**, chopped

3/4 cup chopped **celery**

1 tablespoon **chili powder**

1 1/2 cups fresh **mushrooms**, chopped

1 (28 ounce) can chopped whole peeled **tomatoes** with liquid

1 (19 ounce) can **kidney beans** with liquid

1 (11 ounce) can whole **corn kernel** with liquid

1 1/2 teaspoons dried **basil**

1 1/2 teaspoons dried **oregano**

1 tablespoon ground **cumin**

Directions

In a large pan, heat oil over medium high heat.

Sauté garlic, onions, and carrots until tender, but not mushy.

Add red and green bell peppers, celery and chili powder, stir and cook until half cooked.

Add mushrooms and cook until half cooked. Stir in corn kernels, tomatoes, and kidney beans.

Season the vegetable mixture with oregano, basil and, cumin.

Bring mixture to a boil, cover; simmer in low heat for 20 minutes. Stir occasionally.

Ready to serve!

Nutritional Information: 155 calories; 3 g fat; 29 g; 0 mg cholesterol; carbohydrates; 6.8 g protein; 423 mg sodium.

Paleo Chili

Paleo eaters should not worry when it comes to our chili recipe. It is prepared without beans, yet it is flavorful and saucy. Non-Paleo eaters can add pinto beans to this recipe to satisfy your cravings. Since this is a Paleo recipe, the meat should also be grass-fed.

Servings: 4

Ingredients

1 pound ground **bison**

1/2 pound **spicy ground pork sausage**

1 **chipotle pepper**, dried and stem removed

1 ½ teaspoons **coconut oil**

4 minced **garlic cloves**

1 cup **yellow onion**, chopped

1 cup **green bell pepper**, chopped

1 cup **red bell pepper**, chopped

1/2 teaspoon **black pepper** (ground)

1 can (28 ounces) crushed **tomatoes**

1 cup boiling **water**

1 tablespoon **chili powder**

1 teaspoon **oregano,** dried

1 teaspoon **unsweetened cocoa powder**

1 teaspoon **Worcestershire sauce**

1 1/2 teaspoons **kosher salt**

1 tablespoon ground **cumin**

Directions

In a bowl, soak chipotle pepper in boiling water for 10 minutes, until it softens.

Remove chipotle pepper from boiled water, and mince.

In a deep stock pot, melt the coconut oil on medium heat. Stir in onion, red and green bell peppers until soft for 5 to 10 minutes.

Add garlic and chipotle pepper into the mixture and cook for 1 minute or until it releases a strong aroma.

Add ground bison and sausage into the spice mixture. Stir and cook for 10 to 12 minutes, until meat and sausage are browned and crumbly.

Add chili powder, oregano, cumin, Worcestershire sauce, and cocoa powder into the meat mixture, stirring occasionally.

Add crushed tomatoes, black pepper and salt. Stir mixture and bring to a boil. Simmer over low fire until blended for 10 minutes, stir.

Serve!

Nutritional Information: 380 calories; 17.2 g fat; 90 mg cholesterol;26.4 g carbohydrates; 33 g protein; 1567 mg sodium.

CORN CHILI

Corn is a good substitute for carbohydrates that is less in sugar content. When used as an ingredient for chili recipes, it leaves a tangy taste to your palate. This recipe is best served with corn bread or pasta with cheddar cheese as topping.

Servings: 6

Ingredients

2 tablespoons **vegetable oil**

1 diced **onion**

1 pound frozen **corn kernels**

2 cans (14.5 ounces) **Mexican-style stewed tomatoes**

1 can (15 ounces) drained **pinto beans**

1 teaspoon ground **cayenne pepper**

2 teaspoons dried **oregano**

1 can of (15 ounces) drained **kidney beans**

2 teaspoons **chicken bouillon granules**

¼ teaspoon ground **black pepper**

1 ½ cups **tomato sauce**

2 tablespoons **tomato paste**

1 cup **water**

½ teaspoon **salt**

Directions

Stir fry onion in a large pot over medium heat for 1 minute.

Add oregano and cayenne, stir and cook for 1 minute.

Stir in tomatoes, corn, kidney and pinto beans.

Add chicken bouillon granules, water, pepper, salt, and tomato paste and tomato sauce.

Cook the mixture, uncovered, until becomes slightly consistent, stir occasionally and cook for 10 to 15 minutes.

Enjoy!

Nutritional Information: 391 calories; 6.6 g fat; 1 mg cholesterol;70.9 g carbohydrates; 18.7 g protein; 1310 mg sodium.

CHILI DIP

Chili dip is versatile in the like that it goes well with any type of events, and gatherings. It is very simple and less costly. Serve it with your tortilla or chips.

Servings: 32

Ingredients

1 package (8 ounces) softened **cream cheese**

1 can of (15 ounces) **chili without beans**

1 can (10 ounces) drained and diced **tomatoes with green chili peppers**

Directions

Combine cream cheese, diced tomatoes with green chili peppers and chili without beans in a medium size microwave safe bowl.

Microwave the tomato-pepper mixture on high temperature for 1 minute.

Remove mixture from microwave. Stir and repeat until it becomes hot and well blended.

Enjoy!

Nutritional Information: 37 calories; 2.8 g fat; 10 mg cholesterol 1.5 g carbohydrates; 1.5 g protein; 110 mg sodium.

CHEESY CHILI ENCHILIDAS

Chili and cheese are perfect combination to come up with this delicious treat for tailgating and get-together.

Servings: 10

Ingredients

1/4 cup **vegetable oil**

1 small chopped **onion**

1 package (10 ounces) **corn tortillas**

1 package (16 ounces) grated **Cheddar cheese**

2 cans (19 ounces) **chili without beans**

1 package (8 ounces) cubed **processed cheese**, divide into two

Directions

Preheat oven at 350 degrees Fahrenheit. Prepare a 9 x 13 baking dish and grease.

In a skillet, heat oil. Dip the tortillas individually into the hot oil and turn each side. Set aside.

Sprinkle evenly the Cheddar cheese on one side of the warmed tortilla.

Roll the tortillas to enclose cheese. Place the cheese-filled tortillas in the baking dish, seam facing down.

In a deep bowl, combine half of the processed cheese, onion and chili.

Pour the mixture on top of the tortillas. Sprinkle the remaining processed cheese on top of tortillas.

Bake in the preheated oven for 20 minutes until bubbly.

Serve!

Nutritional Information: 525 calories; 36.5 g fat; ; 89 mg cholesterol; 24.1 g carbohydrates; 26.6 g protein; 1178 mg sodium

Buffalo Chickpea and Bulgur Chili

Vegetarians will love this chili treat. It is super easy to do and does not take longer to have your tastiest chili in town.

Servings: 2-4

Ingredients

1 medium minced **onion**

1 tablespoon **olive oil**

1/4 cup **bulgur**

1 1/2 cups **chickpeas**

1/2 cup **Frank's red hot**

2 cups **stewed tomatoes**

1 cup **vegetable broth**

2 teaspoons **smoked paprika**

1/2 teaspoon **salt**

Directions

In a skillet, heat oil over medium heat. Stir in onion until translucent for 5 to 6 minutes.

Add bulgur, vegetable broth and stewed tomatoes, stir and bring to a boil.

Simmer mixture over low temperature for 10 minutes.

Add the chickpeas, smoked paprika, Frank's red hot, and salt. Cook for 10 to 15 minutes until bulgur is soft.

Pour additional vegetable broth and adjust salt, stir and continue cooking until mixture is consistent.

Serve chili in individual broiler-safe bowls, and top with blue cheese and croutons.

Place them under broiler and allow the cheese to melt.

Enjoy!

Nutritional Information: 367 calories;17 g protein; 59.7 g carbohydrate; 8.5 g fat; 0 mg cholesterol; 326 mg sodium.

BLACK BEAN SWEET POTATO CHILI

This one is great for your health. The sweet potato tastes better than simply boil them. Diabetics can now enjoy a delicious chili with this flavorful treat.

Servings: 4

Ingredients

1 tablespoon and 2 tsp. **extra-virgin olive oil**

1 large diced **red onion**

4 minced **cloves garlic**

1 medium-large peeled and diced **sweet potato**

2 tablespoons **chili powder**

½ teaspoon **chipotle pepper,** ground

½ teaspoon **cumin,** ground

3 ½ cups **vegetable stock**

1 can of (15 ounces) rinsed **black beans**

1 can of (14.5 ounces) diced **tomatoes**

½ cup **quinoa,** dried

4 teaspoons **lime juice**

1/4 teaspoon salt

Directions

In a large, deep saucepan, heat 1 tablespoon plus 2 teaspoons of oil over medium high heat.

Add in sweet potato and onion, stir and cook until onion is translucent for 5 minutes.

Stir in garlic, chipotle pepper, chili powder, salt and cumin.

Add in the vegetable stock, black beans, quinoa, and tomatoes and bring mixture to a boil. Stir until mixture is blended.

Cover the saucepan and simmer the mixture over low fire.

Cook the mixture until the quinoa and sweet potatoes are tender, and the mixture is consistent.

Pour in lime juice. Remove the saucepan from the fire.

Garnish chili with cheese, avocado, cilantro or cream before serving.

Enjoy!

Nutritional Information: 978 calories, 48.4 g protein, 176.4 g carbohydrate, 13.4 g fat ; 0 mg cholesterol, 271 mg sodium.

BUTTERNUT SQUASH CHIPOTLE CHILI WITH AVOCADO

If you dislike meat, this recipe is for you. All types of vegetarians can enjoy a sumptuous treat with this unique blend of butternut squash, beans, and chili topped with avocado.

Servings: 4

Ingredients

2 tablespoons **olive oil**

1 medium chopped **red onion**

4 minced **garlic cloves**

2 chopped **red bell peppers**

1 small or 1 ½ pounds **butternut squash**

1 tablespoon **chili powder**

½ tablespoon chopped **chipotle pepper in adobo**

1 teaspoon ground **cumin**

¼ teaspoon ground **cinnamon**

1 **bay leaf**

2 cans (15 ounces each) drained and rinsed **black beans**

1 small can (14 ounces) **diced tomatoes with liquid**

2 cups **vegetable broth**

Pinch of **salt**

2 **avocados**, diced

3 corn tortillas for crispy tortilla strips

Directions

Peel butternut squash and chop into ½ inch cubes. Set aside.

Heat over medium fire the olive oil in a 4 to 6 quart stockpot or Dutch oven until shimmering.

Add onion, bell pepper and chopped butternut squash. Cook and stir until onions are translucent.

38

Reduce heat to medium low and stir in garlic, ½ tablespoon chopped chipotle peppers, chili powder, cinnamon, and cumin.

Stir regularly until aroma is released for about 30 seconds.

Add bay leaf, black beans, and tomatoes with liquid, and vegetable broth.

Stir well to combine ingredients. You can add more chipotle peppers, remove the bay leaf and add more salt.

Continue cooking until the squash is tender and the liquid is reduced.

For the tortilla strips:

Stack the tortillas and slice into thin strips, about 2 inches x ¼ inches.

In a skillet, heat a few amount of olive oil over medium heat and toss in the sliced tortillas.

Sprinkle them with salt and turn until crispy and golden brown, for 4 to 7 minutes.

Using tongs remove the tortilla strips and drain using a paper towel in a plate. Serve the chili in bowls.

Top them with tortilla strips and diced ripe avocado or cilantro or red pepper flakes.

Enjoy!

Nutritional Information: 591 calories; 23.9 g fat; 0 mg cholesterol; 84 g carbohydrates; 20.3 g protein; 1069 mg sodium.

CHAPTER 4: CHICKEN
CREAMY WHITE CHILI

Try this super yummy chili to keep stress away. Simply done, but the taste is unbelievable.

Servings: 8

Ingredients

1 tablespoon **olive oil**

1 pound deboned and skinless **chicken breast** halves, cut into ½ inch cubes

1 chopped **onion**

2 cloves chopped **garlic**

2 cans (15.5 ounces) drained Great Northern **beans**

1 can (14.5 ounces) **chicken broth**

2 cans (4 ounces) chopped **green chilies**

½ cup heavy **whipping cream**

1 cup **sour cream**

¼ teaspoon **cayenne pepper**

½ teaspoon ground **black pepper**

1 teaspoon ground **cumin**

1 teaspoon dried **oregano**

1 teaspoon **salt**

Directions

In a large saucepan, heat oil over medium heat.

Stir in chicken, garlic, and onion, and cook for 10 to 15 minutes, until middle of chicken is no longer pinkish.

Add drained and rinsed beans, chicken broth, cumin, green chilies, salt, black pepper, cayenne pepper, and oregano.

Stir and bring to a boil. Simmer for 30 minutes in low fire.

Remove chili mixture from the fire. Stir in heavy whipping cream and sour cream until blended.

Enjoy!

Nutritional Information: 334 calories; 15.1 g fat; 63 mg cholesterol;   29.7 g carbohydrates; 21.3 g protein; 888 mg sodium.

QUESO CROCKPOT CHICKEN CHILI WITH ROASTED CORN AND JALAPEÑO

Enjoy a relaxing weekend with this flavorful blend of chicken breasts, salsa, corn, and black beans that is so creamy and yummy. Thanks to the infusion of light cream cheese and the Pepper Jack cheese.

Servings: 8

Ingredients

1 pound skinless and boneless **chicken breasts**

3 cups **salsa**, divide into 2

1 teaspoon **cumin**

2 teaspoons **chili powder**

3 minced **bell peppers**

1 1/2 cups **water**

1 can (14 ounces) drained and rinsed **corn**

6 ounces Pepper **Jack cheese**

1 minced **jalapeno pepper** (seeds and ribs removed)

1 can (14 ounces) drained and rinsed **black beans**

4 ounces **light cream cheese**

1/2 teaspoon **salt**

Topping:

Cilantro

Blue corn tortilla chips for dipping

Directions

In a crackpot, place chicken breast, water, 1 ½ cups salsa, chili powder, salt and cumin.

Cover and cook on low temperature for 6 to 7 hours or on high temperature for 3 to 4 hours.

Shred the chicken when cooked using two forks directly in the crackpot, make sure it is not too hot to handle.

Using paper towel, pat dry the minced peppers.

Place bell peppers in a nonstick skillet without oil over high heat, cook for 4 to 5 minutes without touching them to create a roasted appearance.

Stir the peppers until they turn brown and set aside. Do this process with the jalapeno and corn.

Add the roasted corn, jalapeno and bell peppers to the shredded chicken meat.

Add remaining salsa, cream cheese and black beans to the mixture, stir and replace the cover. Give time to melt the cream cheese. You may adjust the chili consistency by adding ½ cup water.

Simmer the soup for 15 to half an hour until the mixture is melted and consistent.

Add the Pepper Jack cheese to the chili before serving.

Serve!

Nutritional Information: 327 calories;15.1 g fat; 76.8 mg; cholesterol;24.3 g carbohydrates; 1124 mg sodium; 24.2g protein.

Southwest chicken chili

Try this chicken chili with pinto beans and heavy cream. It makes you dance with its creaminess! This chili is a real treat for your weekend event.

Servings: 6

Ingredients

3 to 4 cups shredded cooked **chicken**

3 tablespoons **butter**

2 cans drained and rinsed **pinto beans**

1 medium diced **onion**

1 medium diced **green pepper**

2 minced **garlic cloves**

1 cup **corn**

1 diced **jalapeno peppers** (remove seeds and ribs)

2-1/2 teaspoons **Kosher salt**

2 tablespoons **tomato paste**

3-4 cups **chicken broth,** divided

3/4 cup **heavy cream** or **whole milk**

3 tablespoons **flour**

4 teaspoons **Ancho chili powder**

2 teaspoons **cumin**

Toppings:

Torn **cilantro**

Sour cream

Torn **cilantro**

Crushed **tortilla chips**

Pepper Jack Cheese

Directions

Heat butter over medium-low heat in a Dutch butter, and sauté the onions, garlic, green pepper, and jalapenos.

Season spices with the cumin and Ancho chili powder when they become soft.

Drizzle spices with flour and stir to incorporate. Cook mixture for one minute.

Pour the heavy cream or milk, and one cup of the chicken broth. Stir and simmer.

Add in tomato paste, stir and add the beans, chicken and corn. Stir mixture, cover and simmer for 45 minutes to 1 hour over medium low fire.

Remove the lid of the Dutch oven and let mixture simmer for another 15 minutes.

Serve chili with crushed corn tortilla chips, torn cilantro and sour cream or Pepper Jack Cheese.

Enjoy!

Nutritional Information: 236 calories;14.9 g fat; 4.9g carbohydrates; 69 mg cholesterol, 355 mg sodium; 19.5 g protein.

CHAPTER 4: PORK
OKTOBERFEST CHILI

Have a taste of real German pork sausage with this recipe, which adds a festive mood in October, even if you are in the comfort of your home.

Servings: 14

Directions

2 ½ pounds fresh **bratwurst links**, 1 inch slices

2 tablespoons **bacon drippings**, divide into two

1 large diced **onion**

1 diced green **bell pepper**

2 diced **jalapeno peppers**

4 minced **garlic cloves**

2 cups drained **sauerkraut**

2 cans (15 ounces) drained **red beans**

2 cans (15 ounces) petite diced **tomatoes**

1 can (28 ounces) crushed **tomatoes**

2 cans (15 ounces) **tomato sauce**

2 cans (12 ounces) **tomato juice**

1 can (12 ounces) or bottle **German-style beer**

1 tablespoon **salt**

3 tablespoons **white sugar**

2 teaspoons **garlic powder**

2 teaspoons **paprika**

1 teaspoon **allspice**

1 teaspoon **oregano**

1 tablespoon **black pepper**

1 tablespoon **cumin**

1/4 cup chili **powder**

2 1/2 ounces **milk chocolate candy**

Directions

In a large skillet, place the sliced bratwurst and 1 tablespoon bacon drippings.

Cook and stir over medium heat until browned and pink color is gone for about 15 minutes. Remove excess oil.

In a large, deep pot, place 1 tablespoon of bacon drippings and cook over medium heat.

Stir in onion, jalapeno and green peppers, and garlic until onion is soft for 8 minutes.

Add bratwurst with the vegetable. Cook and stir.

Add the sauerkraut, petite diced tomatoes, red beans, crushed tomatoes, tomato juice, beer, tomato sauce, and stir.

Add salt, cumin, black pepper, chili powder, garlic powder, sugar, oregano, allspice and paprika, and stir.

Bring chili mixture to a boil. Simmer in low fire.

Add the milk chocolate until dissolved. Simmer for another 5 hours, stirring mixture occasionally.

Enjoy!

Nutritional Information: 451 calories; 26.8 g fat; 52 mg cholesterol; 36.2 g carbohydrates; 16.6 g protein; 2226 mg sodium.

50

Chapter 5: seafood
Lobster Chili

Love seafood? This recipe is created to satisfy seafood lovers who want a dish that is creamy with a strong aroma of lobster and chili.

Servings: 4

Ingredients

2 tablespoons **olive oil**

2 small or **chicken lobsters**

1 diced **onion**, divide into two

2 cloves **garlic**

1 diced **carrot**

4 **stalks celery**, diced

1 **bay leaf**

2 cups **Great Northern Beans**

2 tablespoons **chili powder**

1 teaspoon ground toasted **cumin**

1/2 cup **heavy cream**

1 tablespoon chopped fresh **cilantro**

3 quarts **water**

Salt to taste

Cracked pepper

Directions

Place half of the diced celery, onion and carrot in a large stock pot. Add the peppercorns, bay leaf and water, bring to a boil.

51

Add the lobster into the pot; let it simmer for 15 minutes. Remove boiled lobster, strain and set aside the lobster broth.

In a large skillet, heat olive oil on medium heat. Sauté the remaining diced onion, carrot and celery and garlic, stir fry.

Add water, cumin, chili powder, and beans. Cover and cook until beans are soft for 45 minutes.

Remove the lobster from the shell. Rough chop and add lobster to the soup.

Add cilantro and cream. Season the chili with pepper and salt.

Enjoy!

Nutritional Information: 222 calories; 14g fat; 116 mg cholesterol; 466 mgs; 10.98 g carbohydrate; 14.85g protein.

CONCLUSION

Thank you so much for downloading this eBook. We at Savour Press hope that this cookbook has provided you insights on how to prepare chilis. This eBook is composed of a curated list of the most easiest and delicious 20 chili recipes that you can begin with. These recipes are categorized into beef chili, chicken chili, veggie chili, turkey chili, and pork and lobster chilis. This is to make sure that you have no reason why you cannot prepare chili if you are on a restricted diet or because of your religion. We at Savour want everybody to enjoy our recipes, and they are easy to prepare not to mention the availability of the ingredients. There is no reason to fuss when your friends will pay you a surprise visit, this book offers what you want to make your chilis super yummy, stress-free and cost saving.

We hope you will have much fun preparing these recipes.

Thanks again for your support.

Happy Cooking!

Made in the USA
Monee, IL
09 November 2021

81756424R00031